JUST MAKE A DIFFERENCE

LEADING UNDER PRESSURE

RON HARVEY

JUST MAKE A DIFFERENCE: Leading Under Pressure

Copyright © 2017 Ron Harvey

All rights reserved. No part of this book may be reproduced or transmitted in any form or by any means, electronic or mechanical, including photocopying, recording, or by any information storage and retrieval system, without permission in writing from the copyright owner.

ISBN: 978-0692879764

Library of Congress Control Number: 2017917431

Global Core Strategies and Consulting, LLC Columbia, SC

www.GCS.Consulting

"HAVING THE ABILITY TO LEAD UNDER PRESSURE WILL BE THE DIFFERENCE BETWEEN BEING A GREAT LEADER AND A GOOD LEADER."

JUST MAKE A DIFFERENCE: Leading Under Pressure

"IF YOU WANT OR NEED HELP FROM OTHERS, LET THEM KNOW BY ASKING FOR THEIR HELP AND EMBRACING THEIR HELP."

www.GCS.Consulting

JUST MAKE A DIFFERENCE: Leading Under Pressure

"IF YOU DON'T HAVE SOMETHING TO MEASURE YOUR GROWTH, YOU WON'T BE SELF-AWARE OR INTENTIONAL ABOUT YOUR GROWTH."

JUST MAKE A DIFFERENCE: Leading Under Pressure

"WHATEVER SUCCESSFUL PEOPLE KNOW, THEY SOUGHT SOMEONE OUT TO LEARN IT FROM."

www.GCS.Consulting

JUST MAKE A DIFFERENCE: Leading Under Pressure

"IT'S NOT WRONG TO LACK KNOWLEDGE; IT'S WRONG TO THINK YOU KNOW ALL OF THE ANSWERS."

"KEEPING YOUR HEAD IN THE GAME FOR THE ENTIRE GAME, GIVES YOU A BETTER CHANCE TO DO WHAT SEEMS IMPOSSIBLE."

> "WINNERS STAY FOCUSED, CONFIDENT, COMMITTED, AND ADAPTIVE."

JUST MAKE A DIFFERENCE: Leading Under Pressure

"BECOME A LEADER THAT THE PEOPLE TRULY TRUST, AND THEN YOU CAN LEAD THEM."

www.GCS.Consulting

"PEOPLE WILL BUY INTO YOUR VISION WHEN THEY BELIEVE YOUR CHARACTER AS A LEADER."

JUST MAKE A DIFFERENCE: Leading Under Pressure

"CHARACTER MATTERS MORE THAN KNOWLEDGE WHEN PEOPLE DECIDE TO FOLLOW YOU."

www.GCS.Consulting

"MAKE SURE YOUR AUDIO MATCHES YOUR VIDEO… DISPLAY WHAT YOU SAY…"

JUST MAKE A DIFFERENCE: Leading Under Pressure

"BUILD A TEAM," BECAUSE THEY WILL ALWAYS OUTPERFORM INDIVIDUALS."

www.GCS.Consulting

> "LIFE HAPPENS TO ALL OF US, AND WE ALL HAVE CHOICES ON HOW TO RESPOND EFFECTIVELY."

JUST MAKE A DIFFERENCE: Leading Under Pressure

"STOP COMPLAINING BECAUSE RARELY DOES IT HELP IMPROVE OUR ATTITUDE OR SITUATION."

www.GCS.Consulting

> "LIFE DOES HAPPEN AND WHEN IT DOES, GO THROUGH IT, PRAY THROUGH IT, GROW THROUGH IT…"

JUST MAKE A DIFFERENCE: Leading Under Pressure

"PEOPLE CATCH MORE FROM WHAT THEY SEE THAN WHAT THEY HEAR, SHOW WHAT RIGHT LOOKS LIKE EVEN WHEN THE CAMERA IS OFF."

www.GCS.Consulting

> "THE WRONG ATTITUDE WILL MAKE THE BEST IDEAS AND STRATEGIES FAIL."

JUST MAKE A DIFFERENCE: Leading Under Pressure

> "WHAT IS IN YOUR HEART WILL SHOW UP; MAKE SURE YOUR HEART IS RIGHT."

www.GCS.Consulting

"TAKE THE OPPORTUNITY TO BE INTENTIONAL ABOUT ADDING VALUE TO OTHERS."

JUST MAKE A DIFFERENCE: Leading Under Pressure

"IF YOU REALLY WANT TO CHANGE YOUR SITUATION, THEN YOU MUST BE WILLING TO IMPROVE WHO YOU ARE AS A PERSON."

JUST MAKE A DIFFERENCE: Leading Under Pressure

> "YOU DON'T GET BETTER JUST BECAUSE YOU LIVE LONGER, BUT YOU SHOULD STRIVE TO GET BETTER THE LONGER YOU LIVE."

JUST MAKE A DIFFERENCE: Leading Under Pressure

"YOU MUST BE INTENTIONAL ABOUT YOUR PERSONAL AND PROFESSIONAL GROWTH."

www.GCS.Consulting

"GROWTH IS NOT COMFORTABLE WHEN YOU ARE GOING THROUGH IT, BUT IT IS VERY REWARDING ONCE YOU ACHIEVE IT."

JUST MAKE A DIFFERENCE: Leading Under Pressure

"PATIENCE ALLOWS YOU TO GROW DURING EACH MOMENT."

www.GCS.Consulting

"EMBRACING FEEDBACK DOES NOT MEAN WE LOSE OURSELF; IT ALLOWS US TO IMPROVE OURSELF."

> "EVERYTHING IN LIFE GOES THROUGH A PROCESS TO BE DEVELOPED, TO CHANGE, AND TO GROW."

JUST MAKE A DIFFERENCE: Leading Under Pressure

"BE AUTHENTIC IN ALL THAT YOU DO, BECAUSE PEOPLE DESERVE THE BEST."

JUST MAKE A DIFFERENCE: Leading Under Pressure

"BE PATIENT, BECAUSE CHANGE DOESN'T COME AT YOUR PACE."

www.GCS.Consulting

> "ENJOY THE JOURNEY, ENJOY THE PEOPLE, AND ENJOY THE EXPERIENCE."

JUST MAKE A DIFFERENCE: Leading Under Pressure

"BE INTENTIONAL ABOUT EVERYTHING YOU DO OR DON'T DO!"

www.GCS.Consulting

"YOU DON'T ACHIEVE THE GREATEST RESULTS WITH A HALF THOUGHT OUT PLAN."

JUST MAKE A DIFFERENCE: Leading Under Pressure

"YOU GET TO YOUR DESTINATION BY PLANNING AND EXECUTING WHAT IS REQUIRED EVERY DAY."

> "ACHIEVING YOUR BEST IS GOING TO REQUIRE YOU TO BE MORE INTENTIONAL ABOUT WHAT YOU ARE DOING AND WHAT YOU STOP DOING."

JUST MAKE A DIFFERENCE: Leading Under Pressure

"YOUR REWARD CAN BE GREATER IF YOU ARE MORE INTENTIONAL ABOUT YOUR PROCESS."

www.GCS.Consulting

"YOUR IMAGINATION IS MORE POWERFUL THAN YOUR KNOWLEDGE."

"THE ABILITY TO THINK BEYOND YOUR CURRENT SITUATION OR CIRCUMSTANCES IS REQUIRED TO ACHIEVE MORE THAN WHAT YOU CAN SEE TODAY."

> "BE CREATIVE IN YOUR THINKING, STOP ALLOWING YOURSELF OR OTHERS TO PUT YOU, YOUR IDEAS, OR YOUR DREAMS INTO A BOX."

JUST MAKE A DIFFERENCE: Leading Under Pressure

"THE BEST IDEAS STARTED WITH SOMEONE THINKING DIFFERENTLY AND COURAGEOUSLY."

www.GCS.Consulting

> "YOU DON'T WIN THE GOLD MEDAL WITH A FEW NIGHTS OR DAYS OF INTENSIVE TRAINING."

JUST MAKE A DIFFERENCE: Leading Under Pressure

"SUCCESS OFTEN COMES AFTER YOU HAVE GONE THROUGH SOME STRUGGLES."

www.GCS.Consulting

> "SOMETIMES THE BEST WAY TO HELP SOMEONE YOU CARE ABOUT IS TO HOLD THEM ACCOUNTABLE."

JUST MAKE A DIFFERENCE: Leading Under Pressure

"GIVE PEOPLE A HAND-UP, NOT A HAND- OUT. ALLOW THEM TO KEEP THEIR DIGNITY AND BE A PART OF THEIR RESCUE."

www.GCS.Consulting

> "STOP SHRINKING BACK TO SAFETY AND SURGE FORWARD TO SUCCESS."

> "DON'T HAVE SELF-LIMITING BELIEFS ABOUT WHAT YOU CAN DO AND HOW MUCH YOU CAN ACCOMPLISH."

> "KNOWING WHO YOU TRULY ARE CAN FREE YOU UP FROM BEING WORRIED ABOUT ALL OF THE LABELS AND TITLES THAT OTHER PEOPLE OFTEN ASSIGN TO YOU."

"YOUR SELF-WORTH DOES NOT COME FROM OTHERS, SO STOP ALLOWING IT TO DETERMINE WHO YOU ARE OR WHAT YOU WILL BECOME."

> "BE HONEST ABOUT YOUR POTENTIAL AND RECOGNIZE YOUR LIMITATIONS, SO YOU CAN ENGAGE THE RIGHT PEOPLE TO ADD VALUE TO YOU."

JUST MAKE A DIFFERENCE: Leading Under Pressure

"STOP BEING A STRANGER TO YOURSELF, BE WHO YOU WERE MEANT TO BE."

www.GCS.Consulting

JUST MAKE A DIFFERENCE: Leading Under Pressure

"DON'T JUST THINK OUTSIDE OF THE BOX, RE-CREATE THE BOX."

www.GCS.Consulting

JUST MAKE A DIFFERENCE: Leading Under Pressure

"SOMETIMES YOU HAVE TO HELP FIX THINGS THAT SOMEONE ELSE BROKE."

www.GCS.Consulting

JUST MAKE A DIFFERENCE: Leading Under Pressure

"SUCCESS IS NOT ALWAYS EASY, BUT IT IS ALWAYS ACHIEVABLE IF YOU DETERMINE WHAT IT IS FOR YOU."

www.GCS.Consulting

JUST MAKE A DIFFERENCE: Leading Under Pressure

"EVERYTHING STARTS WITH THE FIRST STEP AND THE COMMITMENT TO SEE IT THROUGH."

www.GCS.Consulting

> "STAY FOCUSED AND ALLOW YOUR DREAMS TO BE BIGGER THAN YOUR CONCERNS."

JUST MAKE A DIFFERENCE: Leading Under Pressure

"STOP COUNTING YOUR LOSSES AND START COUNTING YOUR LESSONS."

www.GCS.Consulting

> "YOUR WILLINGNESS TO STAY THE COURSE IS JUST AS IMPORTANT AS THE DECISION TO START."

JUST MAKE A DIFFERENCE: Leading Under Pressure

"CHECK YOUR ATTITUDE DAILY, BECAUSE IT IS EASY TO GET OFF TRACK AND NOT EVEN NOTICE IT."

"IF YOU REMAIN THE SAME, YOU EVENTUALLY BECOME IRRELEVANT BECAUSE CHANGE IS HAPPENING AND YOU MAY BE LOSING YOUR LEARNING EDGE OR CAPACITY TO KEEP PACE WITH WHAT IS ESSENTIAL."

JUST MAKE A DIFFERENCE: Leading Under Pressure

"DON'T LOSE, BECAUSE YOU REFUSE TO ADAPT TO WHAT IS NECESSARY."

www.GCS.Consulting

> "YOUR TRUE TRANSFORMATION STARTS WITH IMPLEMENTATION, WHICH HAS THE POTENTIAL TO CHANGE YOUR SITUATION."

JUST MAKE A DIFFERENCE: Leading Under Pressure

"STOP ASKING HOW LONG IT'S GOING TO TAKE AND START BELIEVING HOW FAR YOU CAN GO…"

www.GCS.Consulting

www.ingramcontent.com/pod-product-compliance
Lightning Source LLC
Chambersburg PA
CBHW070107100426
42743CB00012B/2673